Around the World

Contents

written by Rachel Walker

In the 16th century, an adventurous young man from Portugal planned to be the first person to sail right around the world. But his motive was not to explore and discover new places, or even to become famous – it was to get rich! Demand for spices sent explorers to the far ends of the Earth in search of exotic spices and the riches they would bring.

500 years ago there was no way to freeze or chill food to keep it from rotting. Unable to use refrigerators or freezers as we do today, people coated their meat in salt to preserve it. They had to use a lot of tasty spices like cinnamon, cloves, nutmeg, and especially black pepper to mask the awful taste of the salted, or often spoiled, meat.

The rich people of Europe would pay almost anything to have their food taste good. With their own climate being too cold and too dry to grow the spices they wanted, they had to search for them elsewhere.

Most spices came
from Indonesia
(known as the Spice
Islands), thousands
of miles from Europe.
Spices were very
expensive because
it was such a long,
risky journey by
ship, with the added
danger of pirates.
The alternative Spice
Trail overland route
was long and slow
too. Camels were
used to cross the
harsh deserts and
steep mountains,
while avoiding attack
by groups of killer
bandits, who tried
to steal the valuable
spices.

Until this time, Europeans had reached the Spice Islands by sailing east, but no one had ever sailed west from Europe to reach the other side of the world. Determined to discover the quickest route to the Spice Islands and be the first to sail around the world, the young Portuguese explorer, Ferdinand Magellan, set sail from Spain in 1519. His fleet of five Spanish ships – the *Santiago*, the *Conception*, the *San Antonio*, the *Trinidad*, and the *Victoria* – carried a crew of 270 men.

The fleet sailed westward from Europe across the Atlantic Ocean until it reached South America. There the crew stocked up with fresh water and food supplies, as well as goods to trade for the spices they wanted, before sailing down the coast to Argentina, looking for a passage through South America.

R DESPAIGNE:
MER OCCANE:
DE CANCER:
MER DES ENTILLES:
LE PERV
LE PERV:
Terre ferme
la conqueste du perou faicte par les espaignols
Canibales
Amazones
Analou
MER DV SV:
AMERIQVE
Amerique ou brefill
Tabajarres
MER DE MAGELLAN:
Riviere de plate
R. PLATE
CAP DE FRIE
Detroit de magellan
11

The voyage was treacherous, and some of the crew, scared and exhausted, rebelled against young Magellan's firm leadership. Magellan dealt with the uprising by executing one of the most mutinous captains and leaving another marooned! His actions showed the crew that mutiny against him was not something they should try! The *Santiago* was sent ahead of the rest of the fleet to explore the route, but a terrible storm blew up, forcing it onto jagged rocks, where it was totally wrecked.

Runaways

More than a year later, in October of 1520, a strait through South America was discovered by accident, when the fleet was sheltering from yet another fierce storm. Despite this success, the crew of the *San Antonio* had lost hope of a successful mission, and forced its captain to turn and flee across the Atlantic and back home to the safety of Spain.

Then only three of the King of Spain's original five ships remained in Magellan's fleet.

It took another month to sail through the dangerous strait before arriving in the Pacific Ocean. There, a journey that they had expected would take only a few days turned into months with no sign of land. The food and water supplies ran out, and the crew had to eat rotten biscuits, chew on leather from the sails, and even eat rats when they could catch them! Three more months went by and many of the crew died of starvation and dehydration. Finally, Magellan and his remaining crew reached Guam, where they were able to eat, rest and recover from their disastrous ordeal.

ATLAN
TICVM
Canariæ
OCEA
OPICVS
17

Disaster

Next, rested and refreshed, they sailed on from Guam, heading for their goal of the Spice Islands and the valuable cargo, nutmeg. But before they could reach it, they were caught in a war between rival kings in the Philippine Islands.

There a group of natives attacked Magellan, killing him with a poisoned arrow in his foot and a spear through his heart. After Magellan was brutally killed, his crew was left with too few men to sail all three ships, so they burned his ship, the *Conception*. With only a small crew and two of the original five ships remaining, they sailed on to the Spice Islands.

Finally, the
surviving men
managed to trade,
loading both ships
with a rich cargo
and setting out
for Spain. On the
way home, the
Portuguese (who
had claimed the
Spice Islands by
then), captured
the *Trinidad* and
stole its cargo of
valuable nutmeg.
The *Victoria* headed
for Spain alone.

Last ship

Almost exactly 3 years after the fleet's original departure, the *Victoria* was the only ship to sail safely back to Spain. Out of the five ships that had begun the journey, only one ship successfully completed the voyage. Out of the original 270 men, only 18 survived the first-ever trip around the world. Although Magellan himself did not complete the voyage, it was his expedition that is recorded in history as the first circumnavigation of the world. Luckily, today, pepper and spices are so common that nobody has to risk their lives to get them!

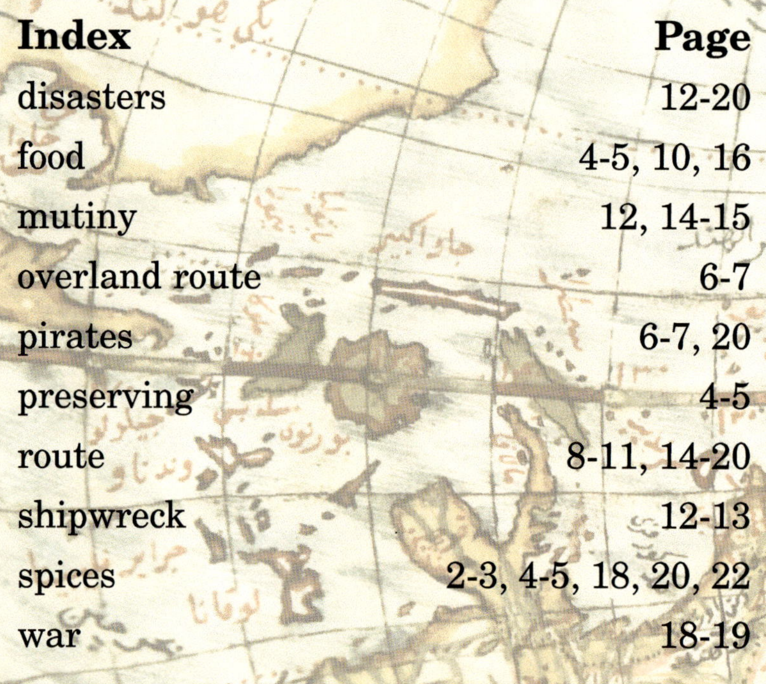

Index	**Page**
disasters	12-20
food	4-5, 10, 16
mutiny	12, 14-15
overland route	6-7
pirates	6-7, 20
preserving	4-5
route	8-11, 14-20
shipwreck	12-13
spices	2-3, 4-5, 18, 20, 22
war	18-19